Expert Terrain

Diane Schenker

Expert Terrain

Poems by Diane Schenker

Word Poetry

© 2023 by Diane Schenker

Published by Word Poetry
P.O. Box 541106
Cincinnati, OH 45254-1106

ISBN: 9781625494344

Poetry Editor: Kevin Walzer
Business Editor: Lori Jareo

Visit us on the web at https://www.wordpoetrybooks.com

*For my two sons
who are the light of my life
and who have lovingly put up with me all these years*

*and to their father, Lawrence James Beck,
who during our time together
taught me so much I didn't know
including how to see*

Acknowledgments

Deep gratitude to the editors and presses who first published these poems, some with revisions:

2 Horatio: "*Nullus Casus Belli*"

Gargoyle: "Poem with No Pants On"

The Gettysburg Review:
"Heirloom"
"In Gratitude to Frank O'Hara Who Came Before"
"Nightmare for Theodore Roethke"
"Observed from the Footpath by the Water"

Pen + Brush In Print::
"Night Land" & "House—Holding"

Relation/Couch/Dreaming (chapbook, Finishing Line Press included the following poems):
"Beast"
"Boolean Search"
"Double Black Diamond"
"Passing"
"Pierre Bonnard, *The Bathroom*, 1932"
"Prognostics of Melancholy"
"Relation/Couch/Dreaming"

RHINO: "*Heimisch*"

Salonzine: "Consider" & "Necessary" (which appeared as "Yes No Yes")

The Community of Writers Poetry Review 2014 (fka: The Squaw Valley Review):
"On Not Knowing"

Subtropics: "Epithalamium" & "Merge and Acquire"

VIA: "The Torment of Saint Anthony"

Writers Bloc: "Dear Marcel" & "Terminal Moraine"

Thanks

My journey into poetry was unexpected and full of surprises. I applied and was rejected, twice, from an MFA program. This opened a marvelous path of many teachers in many places with different environments. All these adventures exposed me to a wonderful range of disciplines and ideas. I call it my University of the Air. So deep gratitude to the many people who taught me, advised me, read my work, gave me feedback, and published my work. Many won't remember me, but I was inspired by and remember them.

Workshop hosts: Poets House; The Gettysburg Review Conference of Writers; Sotto Voce; Fine Arts Work Center, Provincetown; The Poetry Project; Community of Writers at Olympic Valley, CA

Teachers: Suzanne Wise; Peggy Shumaker; Terrance Hayes; Tom Sleigh; Catherine Bowman; Scott Hightower; Marie Ponsot; Dean Young; Stanley Plumly; Carol Frost; Ed Hirsch; Anselm Berrigan; Sidney Wade; Sharon Dolin; Gregory Orr; Sharon Olds; Don Mee Choi; Robert Hass; Harryette Mullen; C.D. Wright; Forrest Gander; Matthew Zapruder; Brenda Hillman

Friends, readers, supporters: Billy Merrell; Lee Rossi; Peter Neil Carroll; Lisbeth Redfield; Barbara Henry

In memoriam:
A very special thank you to Peter Stitt, Founding Editor of *The Gettysburg Review*, who sadly passed away in May 2018. Peter saw something in me and published poems of mine at the very beginning of my journey. His wry, wise presence and tacit support nourished deep roots that led to this book.

Table of Contents

I
In Gratitude to Frank O'Hara Who Came Before............17
Movie Crew at Grand Central Station..............................18
Observed from the Footpath by the Water........................19
Like a Shake of Pepper..20
The Torment of Saint Anthony...21
Prognostics of Melancholy..22
Sonnet to Getting Up Every Day..23
Pierre Bonnard, *The Bathroom* 1932....................................24
Pierre Bonnard, *Cooking Utensils* 1946.................................25
Space—Counter Space..26
Terminal Moraine...27
Nightmare for Theodore Roethke......................................30
In Perpetua..31
Behavioral Game Theory...32
World Without End..33
Necessary...34

II
Take and Fold...37
Epithalamium...38
Argument Against Mirrors...39
Remote Access..40
Flim Flam...42
Apiary of Desire...43
Boolean Search...44
Relation/Couch/Dreaming..46
Beast...47
Heimisch..48
In the Beginning..49
Salt..50
Consider..51
Assay..52
A Kind of Geology...54
Q&A..55

My Sweet Conjunct..56
Foxtrot..57
To the Holder of Grudges..59
Countless..60
Night Land..61
Hate Poem..62
A Measure of Our Days..64
Sweat...66
Poem With No Pants On..68
Double Black Diamond..70
Roadside Turnout—Scenic View Area............................72
Passing..74
Heirloom...75
House—Holding..77
Some Questions...79

III
Merge and Acquire..83
Dear Marcel..84
On Not Knowing...85
I Am Never Ready for This..86
My Name is Martín...88
The Unbanked...90
Visiting Gettysburg National Military Park.....................92
Nullus Casus Belli..95
What the Poem Wants..96
River Song in the Shape of the Hudson..........................98
Incantation for a Bad Day..99
Realization While Trying to Live as a Late 16th c.
    Japanese Warrior...101
Walked into a Bar..103

Notes..105
About the Author..111

I

Now and then it's good to pause in our pursuit of happiness and just be happy.

—*Guillaume Apollinaire*

In Gratitude to Frank O'Hara Who Came Before

Here's to you, Frank O'Hara, all nicotine-
stained fingers and fun.
Go forth! (I have you singing) Go!
Into the hour of lunch. Launch!
Laugh, contemplate, attract!

Oh you *flâneur* of the streets of New York.
Carved marble doorway and dirty cup
crumpled and the lady in furs, fly by
bike guy. Look out! a baby girl's hand,
headline screaming from a fragrant
stack of fresh printed paper. It is lunch!

Let the waist of the day expand. I'll
have some in my cocktail. Crazy elixir,
pigeons and spit. Dance it! Way down
the street till the hour rolls over and
Frank—thank you for lunch!

Movie Crew at Grand Central Station

These real people walk into this real space.
They are making something unreal with their
technologically advanced equipment
and waving hands. A real person walks
into a bar and says this scene is

lacking some essential element Ha Ha Ha.
This other real person's hands gesticulate
No No in that side to side No gesture.
They come and go. They consult their
written things, shaking their heads.

And then there was one.

                              But everyone
has a suitcase. Or lunch. The harness
isn't hooked to anything, as he's
hanging there. One becomes two

in animated conversation. Or is it
a bout of not knowing? Clouds
of impacted wishing scrum
by the egg and dart

in the vaulted ceiling
over the steam table.
Just out of sight.

Observed from the Footpath by the Water

Bird body in air rides a sidewalk all its own
shaping the invisible, each flap of feather, breast
muscle, wings stretching, tilting the notes

that spatter sky, air muscling over this part of the
planet, the whole whistling wild of it clean and indifferent.

Cut clear through, air doesn't bleed. To see it in path, see
the hawk, cream underbelly, riding on opposite space,
unseen seen in swoop, draft, hover, grand cycle ride round.

The unseen felt, every mirror neuron strains to splayed feather,
wings fingering the wind, my own breast swells with flight.

Farther and farther flung, soar goes to spatter wind-scattered
dots, I am a dot, not flying, floored on feet
footing the walk along the water, pronated but looking up

at flecks flying, arched eyebrow or mad flapping towards water
landing with squawks and commotion. My empathy exhausted,

knowledge full of holes, exhausted. Get out of the way, I think,
you will never fly, why watch so wholly? Hard to help,
sing skin and synapses still feeling flight as I trudge

uphill home. Basement windows, hot lint, the smell blowing,
discarded
art, artifacts, mind winding around, around. If I could just spring the
trap.

Like a Shake of Pepper

on an unseasoned page
dark ink carries its prick
meaning prickle like
peppery like sneeze

like the smell of ripe apple
hidden until approached
bitten into the moment
when the sun cracks
the horizon and lights
the trees in theatrical fire—

small instructions in miracles
shine a small light then slide
on—attention turns
to breakfast to the steps
of the day—one + one + one

these small marks—unpack them
as you will, they move the world
        hold on the tongue
                taste revolution.

The Torment of Saint Anthony

> *(Earliest known painting by Michelangelo at 12-13)*

Mad boy meets monsters, outlined black and white.
I can do better than that thinks twelve-year-old
He with fingers straight from god and wild sight.
O! tooth and snarl and fright, the things boys love.

So snicker-snack he's off to fish the stalls,
The piles of shining catch. For sale! But he's
Away to comb his eyes through a boar's hair,
His felty mind inventing hues of fear.

Bland saint corona'd by delicious beasts
so lushly rendered—liver lips, spiked hides
with little thrashing arms, the glistening side
of scales, mouths wide, claws tear, about to feast.

This boy on fire, inventing his own tongue
To speak the world. There was more to come.

Prognostics of Melancholy

> *Prognostics, or signs of things to come, are either good or bad.*
> —Robert Burton

A tree leaps into the landscape from the limning dark,
retools perception. Ground slides sideways, tilting the world.
Reassuring small sounds, without warning, go silent.

Clean sun strikes water, cool slap of air, sadness stays silent.
Heart cracks open to joy that was missing in the dark.
Heron stands; kingfisher flashes all's right with the world.

Head on table, heart in a can spells a fractured world.
The left ear's argument with the right, no matter the agitation, is silent.
My waltz with myself swells in sun and stumbles in the dark.

Dark silence cycles to gold in the all spinning good bad world.

Sonnet to Getting Up Every Day

Did Diane Schenker really do that? Does
she even exist? What other questions come
to mind when all the did nots, mights, suppose-
it-hadn'ts queue up till the brain is numb?

What adds up to a life? Can we discount
the bad decisions or those rude remarks
Diane let fly and too late wished she hadn't?
Both thoughts and acts? The sum is fogged and dark.

Are zigs and zags a fault or do they add?
Proust feared he was just a dilettante
but added up, his life seems not so bad.
Worrying and not doing creates want.

        To clear away the fog it can be said
        Diane stood on two feet and made her bed.

Pierre Bonnard, *The Bathroom* 1932

Slabs, tilts, tesserae of color,
perspective swooning vertical floor in space,
shower of colored geometrical infusion of light,
yellowpink aquamarine, bluish-flavored taste of
cold-tiled wall become textured blushing.

Dreamed world, suspended,
seen beauty, unseen, each stroke of paint
reflects back color on color, each to each,
what a word stands gaping, open-mouthed,
unable to connect to and say—
life bath smell soap light wife.

Bonnard's pink strokes smell touching
sight feeling sweet taste of heart; moist
musk of parted hair, blue-flecked thigh.

Pierre Bonnard, *Cooking Utensils* 1946

Dark colander, dark spoon,
dark pan hang darkly on
the rack for utensils hanging

in the kitchen dark from loss
of light, even the white tiles
leached lightless serving up

the dark utensils quietly hung,
a song of disuse in the kitchen
gone quiet, the light dimming,

sucked to the center of the dark,
oft-handled colander now
still but for our eyes which

over and over travel to its
absence of light right in the
middle, travel back,

forth, slide down and right.
Right there the colored smudge
just barely giving us Pierre

who is staring at the same
place we are, we share
the loss of light, waiting.

Space—Counter Space

Space.
Counter space.
Point.
Counter point.
Object.
Counter object.
Thing.
Counter thing.
Price.
Counter price.
Debt.
Counter debt.
Think.
Counter think.
Sink.
Counter sink.
Yell.
Counter yell.
Weep.
Counter weep.
Give.
Counter give.
Take.
Counter take.
Get.
Counter get.
Absent.
Counter absent.
Space.
Counter space.

Confidence.
Counter confidence.
Out.
Counter out.
Win.
Counter win.
Lose.
Counter lose.
Make.
Counter make.
Believe.
Counter believe.
Forget.
Counter forget.
Yield.
Counter yield.
Spare.
Counter spare.
Slice.
Counter slice.
Deny.
Counter deny.
Hit.
Counter hit.
Pale.
Counter pale.
Flee.
Counter flee.
Be.
Counter be.

Stand between space countered edging outside absence
    here we are   so much thought
        not enough   to counter

Terminal Moraine

When balance is maintained between the melting of the lower end of a glacier and its forward advance, the debris is deposited at that point and builds up a heterogeneous mass of the transported material, called the terminal moraine.

Meanwhile . . .

immobilized, here, I,
        in vast creaking, monstrous,
                              frozen mass

[during glaciations, land masses depressed
        by weight of ice,
                still,
                      frozen]

        sapped of will, a forced observer
                of the slowly traveling bodies
                                    around me,

            I also slowly
                travel, so slowly
                      defying human notions
                                    of time.

        Poor brain whizzing along
                exhausted with useless
                          streams subglacial
                                    of

conjecture

                              And slowly being
                                            eroded being slowly

               marked scraped,

                   . . . polished.

                       What complexion when finally I
                                    am released, what shape will I
                                                have been
                                           ground into?

                              When the ice sheet has
                                            receded slowly
                                   roll to one
                              side, rest, bring
                         knees toward chest,

                slowly sit up and
                             look around and
see past time—vast ice.

How long will it take to be able to . . . ?

No thoughts, no feelings, all
                erosion all
                          stone all
                                  naked.

Where will the high points . . . ?

Sandpapered away, who will see
                the striations
             of those passed?

                    Will ease come?
          Or will I no longer
care—

                    Will there be large sandy outwash?
               flat, welcoming space,
            inviting
   to others?

Nightmare for Theodore Roethke

Milky, singular, sticky and sweet,
viscous and runny, leafy, discreet,
smelly and porous, wooden, profane,
razor sharp, flaccid, lush and inane,

sickly and oozing, violent and pink,
granular, insular, bleary, distinct,
smudged and rumpled, gleaming, torn,
taut, incandescent, fluffy and shorn,

outsized and shrunken, swollen, infected,
pristine, stainless, prefab, dissected,
lingual and medial, furry and slick,
knobby, unbroken, burgeoning, sick,

contradictory, confusing, routine and contrite,
mysterious and stifling, only visible at night.

In Perpetua

If this story is circular, where does it begin? a space
I pass through daily with tin hats and a flagon of beer.

A curious aspect of sinks: k is a fixed and c
an arbitrary constant. They still go down the drain.

Dreamed of folding laundry and Carolina Wrens.
Trees, on the other hand, conveniently stand still.

I have taken to watching my skin grow. Unable
to write my own name I have lost myself.

Infection is asymmetrical. What I read is only
what you wish were happening in your

sad, relentless life. Maintaining surfaces
at all costs, the dark sump squeezes. Blood

is just below me leaning on your sweatered shoulder.
Why does lying win out over truth? Interpretation.

Funny how it never comes out as easily as it goes in.
The end of "not now" is a pile of dust. The dead

don't just go away. There's the chest full of what
was—notes, insults, 35mm slides, a gift for error.

Granular irritations keep the megrims at bay.
Death is a soluble problem—just add water.

Behavioral Game Theory

The brain doesn't like ambiguous situations.
When it can't figure out what is happening,
the amygdala transmits fear to the orbitofrontal cortex.

What separates me from this blade of grass? My complicated cortex.
Though I often enjoy complexity of thought, there are situations
when it might be preferable to not know what is happening.

The grass would not have wept as I did at what was happening.
Even though its parenchymatous layer of tissue is also a cortex,
it lacks the convoluted specialization for grief in painful situations.

Happening to cross the grass, cortex held high, I smile and release all
situations to unwind themselves.

World Without End

World walk breathe beyond all bounds birds lift and oh! lift without
lifting, air boundless, oyster it! your world is, oh, it is pretty grand
and one day you can't stop thinking about your mother, thinking
about watching, feeling echo when not to store go you decide
after all your flesh contains the same drainage, you watched
the fading, in all that sunshine, the her in you is measuring
the days many, willing you to pointless shuffle, sink chair
toilet bed a world pinned patterning limits *Sit down—*
you always do too much and now she sits, dust inside
your head, closer picking push back but let's just
sit, let's just chair just chair just really even bed
to bed, let's just lie down, let's sleep, let's just
sleep, shuffle off coils those, to be or not to
isn't a question when sleep sits on your
head choke no speech now bed chair
so clear, close no stop sleep stop
easy it is easier if stop all you
now all stop all world later
without not now a not lie
with end sleep down to
world tired now end
with world out with
without now world
fatigue sleep the
yes I out with
worlds amen
not without
world with
sleep and
and yes
tired I
and
...

Necessary

Now is the winter of our inevitable results, unavoidably determined by prior conditions.

Essential? Absolutely. Logically. Required.

Convention, on the other hand, dictates plenty of things that are none of its business. Poke convention in the eye with a sharp stick.

Effects are not always what they seem. Beware faulty reverse engineering. It only seems logical.

S seh seh seh incessant abscess accede exceed concede proceed recede secede ancestor. S.

So what, that's my motto. So fucking what.

Absolutely essential, needed,

Required—what small, scratchy volume contains the overlap of necessity and love? Will you tell me?

Yes . . . well, um . . . actually . . . oh dammit—hell yes!

II

What we're now striving for was once nearer and truer and attached to us with infinite tenderness. Here all is distance. There it was breath.

—*Rainier Maria Rilke*

Take and Fold

Dear happy monkey beast, please
take this small piece of heaven, different
and sharp, made sweet with rain
that Death tiptoes through, rain of

silk and angels' blood, beautiful
as thunder. Take and fold it as your heart
is folded by a kiss that god and
the devil fight over, and
        in eternity's corner
                there will be
                        Some Trees.

Epithalamium

epi-, at ✢ *thalamos*, bridal chamber
  (see **thalamus**)
    ↓
        1. *Anatomy.* A large ovoid mass of
            gray matter that relays sensory stimuli
            to the cerebral cortex and acts
            in integrative and nonspecific functions.
        2. *Botany.* The receptacle of a flower.
                —*The American Heritage Dictionary*, 3rd Ed.

Heap round the inner chamber with sweet
Smelling flowers, lay out wine and delectables,
Fresh sets of sheets. Blow horns!
Welcome the two ovoid masses
That the sensory stimuli may be relayed
O! Relay! And may acts be integrative
And nonspecific both, rapture
In the receptacle of a flower.
Enter, bride! Enter, groom!
Stamen, pollen-producing filament and anther,
Pistil of stigma, style and ovary—
Celebrate honey bee, hummingbird. Sip.
Flutter and buzz. Let bowls of fruit, cascading
Flowers pillow the chamber of your promise.
May the soft *Now* be always a token
Held in your remembering hands
for the long *Always* carpeting out ahead.
Begin! And begin! Ha! Awakening!

Argument Against Mirrors

Felicitous day, O! mayhap, perchance,
today will roll off the tips of my fingers.
Look at that harvest moon june spoon
swoon in my arms, my beamish boy!

Cataloguing events, you forgot to look up
and notice. The sea is rising, complicating
the coastline measurement problem. Look!
We've gone from two dimensions to a whole

lot of unnamed species, unknowable
events. Carry on, Jeeves! The peach
juice irrepressibly leaves mouth for
chin and destinations beyond. This

shirt remembers history by what stains it.
Do I? Most stains fade but never die.

The face holds a fine calligraphy.
I ignore it—mirrors are a silly invention.

I'd rather look at you than measure, measure—
mayhap, perchance, my prince—take a bite!

Remote Access

*Delete review record record memo off on system review change press 3 press 3 3 press #7 press *7 speak after beep press 5 system plays press 5 to stop press 5 when finished press 0 or hang up.*

Breathless witless where can this go thinking, me
thinking I had it thinking I might
have known but oh no so near so far sneer *fahrt*
       . . . remote.

A kind of bit of thing in the light you see
and then see it again, re-mote.
But you are here and it is over there
       . . . remote.

And I am here and you are there, curled in our
dimensions which seen from afar look like
a straight line, how simple a journey one would think but
up close we go around and around and around never
touching the thing we would most like to approach Zeno's
       arrow to the heart
              . . . of the matter.

Please enter your remote access code.

Blanking palms sweating I'm no wonder I'm thinking
was that James John or John James dammit just
say hello now maybe it will come up in the conversation
the sequence of words carefully avoiding each other
and elaborately encrypted you are standing so close but
       . . . remote
           there is no
               . . . access.

*Enter your remote access code then press 0 press #9 press *9 then enter desired . . .*

desired state, desired situation, desired prospect, desired orifice, desired proximity, desired desire,
lips slightly parted . . .

Flim Flam

Here we go round the mulberry bush where
Every Good Boy Deserves some word
that starts with F, oh sweet mnemonic
device, please don't hang up.

I'll be calling you-ooh-ooh hums
through the good boy's schematics.
The Hunting, the Fire—and it all ends up
in suburbia? Does that seem fair, he asks?

What they don't tell you is that outside
the Rain still falls and the Sun still shines.
Not always in the same order but why
dig a hole you'll never get out of?

Now for that unruly assembly between
your ears, it's good for some things—
but the rattle-bang, flim-flam can
flip the heart like a blue moon of Sundays.

We're not in the right genre and that oil,
that water—how long
do you want to keep shaking?

I'm taking the rain and the sun bit, I'm
going out in the sweetness and light
without my umbrella, because really—

it ain't success, it's not the fall on your ass
but ripe-for-picking, fall-off-the-edge
bam! dance the mad fandango!

Apiary of Desire

The sharp angles of appetite carve themselves space,
neatly camouflaged in the luxe smoothness of
seared scallops and Sancerre, blood rare tuna steak

by candlelight *en plein air*, leaf rustle sirening through
to Mozart and strawberries, standing in a doorway
at whose threshold they choose to tarry.

Limbs beginning to entangle, fingers tentative and sweet,
his honey'd kisses arousing the bees
who accompany them, humming, as she leafily walks him
to the subway for the journey back to his faraway self,
for it is the time and proper thing to do.

She strolls back home riding the hive,
smiling above the bees buzzing at work
creating a surfeit of honey and wax.

Boolean Search

Be aware of the logical order in which words are connected when using Boolean operators: if you use a combination of AND and OR operators in a search, enclose the words to be "ORed" together in parentheses.

(the pinprick, the blade, the knife, which will it be?
an art to wielding each: imperceptible puncture, carve or slice;
without art, a moment of slippage and——hshshp——sharp intake
of breath

just then, while bearding the mussels, the slip, the ooze and drip of red,
the deed done before perception or feeling find conception,
the heart's pain follows after in all its liquid variations

OR

perhaps it is more clinical, well lit and sterile
all stainless steel, sharp as spit, lined up ready-at-hand
shining on the white liner of the stainless pan

you came here, after all, to remove the painful thing
perhaps hard to remember as you lie all exposed and
vulnerable to the scalpel's bright cut, trembling

OR

it was waltzing that took you, spinning, across the threshold
giddy and laughing, feeling as one but in the landscape
on the other side, so suddenly you can't breathe, stand two apart

one stuck in brambles, the other lost in the woods
it is getting dark, bushes rustling with all that is unseen
and nothing is what it appeared to be from the other side)

AND

despite the variations or metaphors for sorrow,
what is it you feel but relief! bright blaze of breath, triumphant
trout, slicing back below, free to ply the stream another day.

Relation/Couch/Dreaming

Graphite surface toothed abrasion smear smudge mark.
Line makes space makes volume makes . . .
Shape makes illusion makes idea makes . . .
    Relation.

Marks scratched rubbed paper. Thigh.
Line around under line. We.
Ground breaks space breaks line. Apart.
    Couch.

Touching not feeling touching feeling.
Once sensate marked lined lifted held forever.
Evocation representation intersection . . . moment in time.
Eye drawn mirror drawing painting equals . . .
    Dreaming.

Beast

When did it become so unappetizing? The carcass,
bones cracked, marrow sucked out, lying on the plate,

wine drunk. Dread keeps walking. The past flings out
its ashy mantle, a quick turn—all is salt and dust.

The young hawk keeps visiting, eye cocked for rat.
Watching, hands full of drought, I laugh at being

the vehicle for others' nightmares. Reaching my fork
towards joy, pain garnishes your plate. *How lovely*—

nightmare complete. *You're welcome.*
I limp home, bloody paw prints in my wake.

Heimisch

Home. Hamlet. Haunt. Hangar: situate.
I slid off its green surface like a mirror sheds spit.
How I loved that dreamed green on a blue sky and
popcorn clouded day, view from the bridge—it would
be mine! I snapped my fingers at things I did not like.

A life built on sand, not watching the tide come in,
heel-pounding dreamer awash, beached, forgetting those
roots in *Breuckelen*, Broken Land, of millinery and starting over,
fur stitched in summer's sweat. *Geh weiter weg!*
How much more away could I get?

The spoked wheel flings landings about its rim then
gasp! air! first breath after thick sleep, dream draining
so quickly there's just a litter of empty envelopes and
accidents. Triangulate from one crash to the next, map it,
          part story,
                    part weather and rock.

Name it home.

In the Beginning

From blow of muscle to blow, limbs crushed through
The now waterless and heaving rose,
Mother of oceans and unplugged vessel, searing
Down the last, thrashing millimeters of
Pounding darkness and suffocating wall
The head comes.
        Shoulders slide
Slipping extruded into day, moving
Like a new-caught fish, we hear
A door closing on one piece of paradise.

The name over the door is engraved with the chisel of our regret.

Listen! Listen! The last fishy vestige of
Watery heaven is cracked away by the cry,
Small lungs fill with daylight and the world bears
New-minted footprints.

        Walking on,
The wisteria blooms by the porch. The dragonfly charts
Angles of meadow in air, not being able to walk. Taxes are paid
And power lines, humming, carry the work of the world.

If there were more hours in the day we might, we think, see
The sound of the unlocked gate, hear the leaves
Fluttering in sunlight around the last forbidden apple.

Salt

We're in the hole of March, colder
than a woe-digger's knee and dark, too.
Who would go out among pale trees
chattering leafless in wind? Stay in.

Measure the temperature with an old bone.
Yep, it looks like grief today, welling up
in particularly fractious formation,
a real nor'easter with squalls and doom.

Lamps on all day. Peer into the hole
to see what's at the bottom. You can't
see the bottom. Sit.

A sad room is a sad thing indeed, O!
Rain fingering the windows, metaphorically or not.
Did those drapes always hang so disconsolately?

Smell of old ashtray creeps along the floorboards,
insinuating itself in the wallpapered air. O!
tangled shade pulls, O! couch uncomfortable
with unhappy pillows and a throw not warm.

Pillow out and fill all the cups, we're
in for a flashing. The round mounds
might give way and there goes lunch.

Rub eyes and there's salt all over the walls.
It will be valuable later. Shall we
lash ourselves to the kitchen sink?
        Take the ride
                eyes wide
                          full-throated keening.

Consider

Consider housekeeping, consider the rain. Consider
the fly dancing on the window. It herky-jerks its
relentless heartbreak of trying to get out.

A fall warbler, feathers weathery dull in post-connubial
anonymity, hard to identify, appears on the seedy

maple stuffing itself for its long flight. Consider
the dirty window. You lift it to see more
clearly. The fly stumbles up with it, then out.

The warbler is gone but you can see the rain, its
needled finery gently wetting the patient, nodding
trees. They gossip in whispers among themselves.

Consider the lifetimes spinning out before you, each
small choice weights in one direction or another:

1) You stare out the window with notebook and
pen, channeling the array of tiny beauties before you.

2) You rummage for bucket, sponge and squeegee,
vinegar? ammonia? the window needs cleaning. You
clean it and the rest of them, too, for you are responsible
and efficient. You take a nap.

3) You stare out the window, on the limb of your
thought of how dirty the window is, it really should
be washed.

Grey tatter grows between you
                         and the real rain.
                                       The notebook lies on the table.

Assay

She licked it.
It was not enough.

Who knew the measure of what
would be a satisfactory amount?

What small god kept the list of ingredients
and measured procedures that graced

the simplest of recipes with predictable
outcomes from her obedient tongue?

She licked it
again, this time

with scientific intent, hoping
for reliable data and a positive

outcome but the measure of things
remained, somehow, despite careful

and scrupulously accurate intervention,
unanswering to her catalogue of needs.

What stood between her and her
blue ribbon fruition, the one-on-one

cloudburst of erupted and well-measured
alchemical production? She sought

the veinous, brackish rippling, barometric
and contrarian, the hydraulic comeuppance,

the one eye with its limpid tear—but the bread
did not rise. The measure of things was perhaps

meant to be the informational
surprise of what was not there.

A Kind of Geology

O Kitchen! O Dust! Things that blow
through the window. Dead leaves,
exhausted city, tree breath, quiet chaos.

O Cooking! O Mystery! the alchemical kind
binding the unexpected to the uninvited—
shed hairs, outside trekked in
combined with a film of frying bacon.

The stove-spatter and the invading drift spawn
brownish raised warts on stove, ceiling and wall—
archipelagos of islands
              unnamed and unnameable.
                                          Atolls
I would wipe off the map by looking.
Strangely present, resistant, sticky and rebellious.
              No soil. No trees.

I would I could sing them down, down
from the walls and ceiling,   sirening them
        down the drain. Instead
              we contemplate each other.

Truce of the tired and the small—
powerfully-armed me, artillery of scrubbers and spray.
Ever-present They—grim grime *guérillas*.

We adjust to proximity—it boils down
        to age-old exhaustion.

Q&A

Q:

What is the question?
Do you want some more mashed potatoes?
Who took the phillips head screw driver
out of the toolbox and didn't put it back?

Which box did you want to open first?
Can I get away with that?
If two cars are both driving to Philadelphia
and one car stops for gas, what time is it?

Can you ask that question in a different way?
Is there enough left in there for me to have some, too?
This thing, right by my eyebrow, does it look weird to you?
Are we there yet? Are we there yet? Are we there yet?

A:

I already told you. No
thanks I couldn't eat another bite.
You know that makes me crazy
when you screw around. Put it back.

Button it up, totally. Hands off.
Just take the goddamn plunge.
Don't think about cars. Forget Philadelphia.
I just don't think Time is a useful concept.

If I've asked you once, I've asked you a thousand times.
I'm really sorry, I ate it all. I already told you
if you don't know, go to the dermatologist.
No. No. Yes. Maybe. I don't think so. No.

My Sweet Conjunct

> ...*Dies süsse Wörtlein: <u>und</u>*
> *(this sweet little word: <u>and</u>)*
>
> —*Tristan und Isolde,* Richard Wagner

"Us" seems not an *and*, not sweet, no matter
how careful my grammatical construct. Clause
       inseparable from clause
              for reasons I do not understand.
Beyond destruction, it is fierce, my *and*.

Foxtrot

Look over there, isn't that Diane Schenker?
Yes, look, it's that face that looks like somebody else's—which
puzzles Diane for she can't see her face no matter how long
she stares, so she keeps extras on hand just in case, slightly
used faces stuffed in her pockets like old tissues.
And doesn't the dust just rise up under her feet
as they meet the pavement, a sudden round
of pigeon-wings as she bursts out from under
the scaffolding doing that crazy dance she loves.
Of course there's the hanging question—
is she too cerebral? Diane Schenker and her big brain
always picking holes in the fabric of the universe.
She picks a hole and falls through it.
       Damn
that's a long way to go and she grabs another
face off the wall as she falls, just in case
some feelings are required or an
exhibition of granite cliffs or
oyster beds that are so damned elusive
even the oysters don't manage to sleep in them.

She keeps a pocket full of stones in the event
that a graceful exit might be in order but of course
that's already been done and mentioning it is so
melodramatic you can see her wince and decide
to go to the grocery store instead. There are always
mouths to be fed and she is a sucker for
Be Prepared. Whose mouth is that anyway
in the middle of her chest, yelling,
while Diane, smiling so graciously on the tightwire,
serves crustless cucumber sandwiches to guests
         she didn't invite?
Diane banged a home right into the forehead of entropy
but there's no one left to bear witness. An opportunity

to start over she exclaimed, rushing off rag in one hand,
instruction manual in the other to the next
windmill, apron strings jerry-rigged as
seat belts for the kids since it would be one
                                              helluva ride.

To the Holder of Grudges

Forgive the evil-doers. Don't hold on,
it's too fine a day. Forgive the tellers
of lies. Forgive the low-liers.

Forgive the high-fliers, the manipulators,
the man in gold chains. Forgive

the smell of fried food coming
from the next table. And the person

eating it. Forgive the steel glass box
jamming up next to the turn-of-the-
century marble sills and ornament.

Forgive the selfish their selfishness,
the psychologists their psychology
applied all hither and yon regardless.

Do not go gentle and rage if you must,
but forgive those who do not. Forgive
what you know. Forgive what you cannot—

the arching trunks, their gracefully twisting
branches that ache over paths, tables
while barely budding out their green mist.

They forgive you your humanity, your
too-swift tick tick tick tick ticking. Heels
clicking down into the subway. The sticking

of habit. One. One. One. One. You need the trees.
Their indifference is your grace. Look up.

Countless

To carry out this test place an index finger or middle finger on the suprasternal notch and palpate. In a young normal person there should be no palpable pulse.

The clock is ticking faster than usual I swear it is loud takes over
the room takes over the pulse beating its tattoo beating the time
it was when flight was a fancy was a loop-the-looping
was what it was all about not a sterile uncoiled dirge.

Older patients will have a noticeable pulse [which] could indicate aging . . .

The sun is shining more brightly than usual making
books drip off the shelves woozy with heat, the contents
sliding out from between the pages to shamelessly sun themselves
as once we did O! California days of decades ago now
speckling the covering behind which we do the arithmetic.

The skin is the largest organ of the human body accounting for about 15 percent of body weight. For the average adult human, the skin has a surface area of between 1.5-2.0 square meters . . . and more than a thousand nerve endings.

The days are running more swiftly than usual panting but sweatless
like dogs—the vertigo of trying to count them sweeps
me horizontal, dreaming—abacus in one hand, calendar in the other

The simplest calendar system just counts days from a reference day. Computations . . . are just a matter of addition and subtraction. Other calendars have . . . multiple larger units of time.

How to count the units in the calculus of mortality?

Night Land

Lying face down in shallows, gills
still pulling in necessary gases
needed for dreaming. Sinking, floating,
out of contact with the land of life.

Here the dead behave in ways
you would not have expected
when you knew them.

Imaginary choices flutter and shift
as you're walking but not walking,
running slowly in thick dream gas.

Someone recommends a small elephant mask
on a stick. Then he is there asking—telling really—
"How is the elephant mask?" Normal,
but impertinent for a dead man.

The suspended animation that passes for a story
continues. Stuck thick—nouns and verbs adhere—
"is" on the edge of someone's lip, the sleeve of your jacket
beworded as though you had leaned on wet paint.

Driving to the next wrinkle, edges of the folds touching,
the meaning lost somewhere far below; your story
eliding from one nonsensical pinnacle to the next.
No one bats an eye. Only later when awake
does the precipitous logic confound your breath.

The dead and the invented still cling to your sleeve,
their grasp slipping faced with sunlight and breakfast.

Hate Poem

I hate you. I hate everything about you. I hate
the smell of things you leave behind when you're not here.
I hate your smiling that is like some other expression entirely. Your laugh—
even worse—water balloons filled with something nasty not water.
      They look funny
              but they're not.
I hate that.

I hate your indifference. I hate your difference. I hate
how I'm caught in between. I hate how I am stuck there,
dodging the fucking not-water balloons. I am filled
with despair. And hate. I hate you so much that naturally

I hate myself. I hate my awkwardness and smells
and those weird little sounds my body parts make
when it's gone silent in the room and everyone can hear.
   I hate that.
      It's all your fault.

If I didn't hate you so much I'd have more time to play pool
or read Proust or learn how to macrame a plant hanger.
I'd settle for a long hot soak in the tub but I hate you so much
I mound myself in front of the TV and drink bourbon and beer.
   Fucking hate.

I should tell you what color the hate is. It's pretty interesting.
It's the kind of thing, when we first knew each other, we would have

talked about for hours, with lips and fingers, spoons forks knives
          in between
                    a whole day untamed amazed
          at the amazingness
                         of how things look
                                   and how we looked at them.

A Measure of Our Days

Clocks are ticking. All sorts. They line shelves
lining walls of rooms and closets, down long halls
                                          Listen.

World of ticking, tocks unsorted
whirr, ding, a choppy stomach-churning sea
of sound, ears can't separate out any harmony
yet a kind of charm in cacophony. What
                          is being measured?
                                      what units marked?

Hands, numbers, circles, squares, minuet, march,
small town band waltzing, tocking, spinning, dawdling
surfeit of measuring, clocks
                          . . . the clocks.

That clock measures time, its pace I've noticed, slowly,
tippily, speeding up like a mediocre drummer
not keeping the beat. I watch its orbit on the wall.

This clock, felt, of bone and all, slowly slowing
unexplaining breaking slowly down, slowing down.
A puzzle. This clock is deeply mine.

I bump into it only seeing the scrapes and bruises later—
How did that get there? Scabbed scrape haunts the back
of my hand taunting me into weeks, waiting.

Waiting. When will the healing finish? When all
expectation is upended, when flesh and bone has grown
into its own dark side. Slightly mocking and ironic

on a good day—when sense of humor hasn't fallen off
its perch, but manages to pick at its moth-eaten plumage,
            flaunting a handsome feather or two.

Sweat

On a certain kind of shirt-sticky day with a kind of smell
of sky tipped full of cumulus and sun, Seattle comes, summer,
hunkered down in a half-built honeymoon house,
the blue tarp roof just an extra sky for laughing and we
fling ourselves above the heads of the ordinary and transform
hubcaps and old prom dresses into new constellations which

light us up as the slick of sweat slaps between us and we make
the world meet us more than halfway. Road trips illuminate the whole
west coast in between openings and openings—wine and cheese!
Applause!
There are babies and breast milk and the goddamn joy comes in
six-packs and dozens at the corner store and it is good! Life uncorks
itself

and who wouldn't want to drink from this fountain filled with what
can't be kept down, designed by the architects of everything
everyone has always wanted, where stamping your feet makes
life rise up like fireworks and shed light where light should be shed.

The sun slips behind a cloud. Boxes in the living room tell rectangular
stories
and phone calls come from a distance the heart hasn't learned to
measure.
Tales of times past hang unprovable as everyone seems to have forgotten
the
verbs for their telling and no one listens much outside their own small
streams.

Night lands with all four feet when the sun goes down. The slick of sweat now
a small serving of hot soup. There are almost never dirty dishes in the sink.

Poem With No Pants On

In the house's temple
she lifts the toilet seat up and down, up and down, admiring
the gleaming white porcelain. "I could serve lunch on this,"
she thinks "and tomorrow, too." A sea change since the presence
of young penises in the house became absence.

O! the things
she had misunderstood, not having a penis herself: sitting
spread-legged on subway seats, writing your name in the snow,
vulnerability of being preceded by your desire (do the Scots
have the right idea wearing kilts?), the very visibility
of one's private parts, no mirror or contortions necessary.

The wiping of the yellow
spots over and over made questions circle around and around
themselves with no answer. What was it about boys peeing?
Was it so much fun that exuberance trumped accuracy?
middle of the night sleepy and can't see? One day, *j'accuse*, it came
out,
face to face with her last young, question hanging casual but bold in
the air.

With a dryness that could suck the yolk out of an egg, a look level
and impassive, "It's backsplash," he said and walked away
as if to say "I am not responsible for Newtonian mechanics."
She left thinking, "You could still wipe it up."

Now her days begin with
patterns stamped like diamond plate on skin, reach for clothes,
door closed, unthinking. The house shouts back, its cache of things,
small hands once attached, now handless, just standing in.
The things shout, too, inviting... Will she? Can she?

She enters the temple, pauses, and does not close the door. Beginning
at the beginning, starting to be adjusting, purposeful, she passes
into the living room smiling and sits down
                              to write this poem
                                              with no pants on.

Double Black Diamond

> *Knowing the ski trail ratings are essential for mountain safety. Double Black Diamonds are used to mark very advanced ski trails that are difficult to ski and have expert terrain.*

Frozen cabled chair bobbles up the mountain. You slide off
above treeline, face of the earth now faceless, dropping
off to nothing, leaving a bowl of sky and death.

In this mortal geography, the breath-suckingly steep
sings—ice music!—brutal, piercing. The world
sways, the gusting waltz pushes you sideways.

The gods of meanness and the gods of envy usually tap
dancing on your spine hold small sway here, everyday language
of deceit an inert jumble, piled, for once, somewhere out of reach.

Truth and death empty the black hole of your mouth; shot of fear
runs
up between your legs, blade slipped just under the ribs.

Elemental terror runs its fingers through your hair. Thoughts
precariously piled, jambled and numb. *Where are*

the snows of yesteryear? Better not to ask or the gods
will tell you; undigested gristle sits lumpen, the price
of freedom amortized over razored years.

Wind-strafed and alone, like blood on ice, you finger
all the old demons. They sit, massive and taunting,
"I dare you," they say. "Be without us if you can."

It's time: you grab the open mouths, squeeze them shut.
Lean down the mountain, *Keep forward,*
keep forward you pray to head off

the ignominious traverse or pathetic
slide on your ass, shaking and in tears. Paradox
grabs your loins—hairs and gorge rise.

In the end, it's so simple. You are looking at your death.
Lean. Just surrender. Fall straight into its arms.

Roadside Turnout—Scenic View Area

Ignorantia juris non excusat

I stand here creaking on the worm-eaten boards of my
mistake-riddled life. Themis, leaning on her double-edged
sword—those scales in her other hand—
looms. Acres sway in the balance.

Did-nots dot the landscape. The view ahead
drops off at the same speed I dare go towards it.
As bits of me quit, the bum knee, squinting at signs,
speed seems like a bad idea. I dither.

"Don't look down," I think. Spurned pork chop recipes—
all my thoughtless, unkind remarks—clothes-pinned
on the line, flap and taunt, the jurisdiction as inescapable
as the damp weight of my ignorance.
I have squandered my ration of excuse.

A young man making his way in the world is sent
on assignment to the Asian office. The girls there
fuss over him, take him to lunch. They only expect
so much of this Western white boy; they are astonished
      when he picks up his chopsticks to eat.
                How is this possible, they ask, you know
                        how to eat with chopsticks?

I look at the dotted landscape of did nots:
    I did not teach them to shave
    I did not teach them to rebuild a carburetor
    I did not teach them to frame a house
        or fix a toaster
Can anyone teach a boy to clean his room?
    I did not.

Here in the nots, the spots and stains, things botched,
                              "My mother taught me," he says,
a small point of surprise, a detail I had forgot.

Passing

Footsteps in rain transmute passage from here to then—
it's the sleeping bread, Mommy, he put it in my mouth.
Grasses yield to flesh yields to bone yields to grasses.

This is the spot. They stood here without calculating the angles
digging struggling unearth out of earth lost music—
trees churning sky despite our heedless, small artifacts.

There was touch once, buttery still,
the pair of them looking, still looking.

The box goes with, the box of words, of delights—
reach across to touch vanished annealings.

Breath times earth equals passing.

Heirloom

Take Medea's cloak of fire.
Put it on. To everyone's great horror,
wearer burns to a crisp.

Take the crisp and crumble
mightily with axe and stone then
mix with shavings of mastodon.

Leave mixture out in the rain until
Time starts being counted, then count:
six epochs and an era or two,

to taste; then mix in a
portion of lake (the best are
too far away to get to easily).

Bring to a boil, then simmer stirring
constantly and with abandon; add
a nuncle and some foolscap sliced

into bite-sized pieces. When soft
and indistinguishable, let cool;
pour into molds, male and female.

When set, remove from molds being
careful to hide any lost limbs; paper
over longing that protrudes through the

surface. Leave adjacent on plate
overnight. The hills and valleys should
be fully populated in the morning; gather

relations together, grind to a fine powder.
Sprinkle over water, let settle then take
the passed-through liquid and spread

over the pasture. Graze the sheep
there, then shear them and make a cloak;
it should be pale in comparison. Do not
wash. Try not to sweat. Wipe up food stains
immediately. Do not dry clean. Hold
the cloak in your mind's eye, in
a storm on the heath, during that bad
land purchase, while your mother is
in the home, during all avoidance of

the problem, then fold carefully making
sure contents do not spill. Put in a Ziplock
bag with moth balls. Tell some stories about it

and of course some jokes. Say
I want you kids to have this.

House—Holding

In layers of soil
and last year's leavings
life insists on itself—

seeds unfold looking
to the light even
on the darkest days

I listen to birds
there is calling, primping, warning
each creature handling

the pressures of spring
with its own clock
and comedy

I, too, wish to build
a house, a holding—
solid, if eccentric, and mine

I pick up board and brick to find
I hold the wet breeze,
the smell of maple blossom and dirt

the world ticks its own
clock—not mine—I push
and collide with my miscalculation

I speak the wrong language—I
stumble my crude two-step with Time's
hand on my waist, mine on its shoulder

"Structure," I think, breathing in
the geology of time passing.

Some Questions

*As for man, his days are as grass, as a flower of the field so he flourisheth.
For the wind passeth over it, and it is gone; and the place thereof*
$$\text{shall know it no more.}$$
$$\text{—Psalm 103}$$

If our days are as grass are we its soil?
Is insignificance a key? Will knowing unlock
       unlooking? unfeeling? unbeing?

Am I asking too many questions? Do words
make any difference to the grass? Are the days
indifferent or precisely filled with meaning?

What did the *place thereof* know before the wind
passed over it? Can a place have knowledge
and be indifferent? Can it know, then not know?

Is not-knowing an absence—or a change
in state I can't put my finger on? Does duration
of knowing affect windspeed, or how long
it takes for the known to become gone?

If we lay together in our grass and the wind
passeth over and we shared place and some
       pretty good laughs
                 and if it is gone
why am I still here thinking about it?

III

Between the idea
And the reality
Between the motion
And the act
Falls the shadow

—*T. S. Eliot, The Hollow Men*

Merge and Acquire

(after e.e. cummings)

The gentle esquires who keep their soft parts boxed
smile as garnish to unbland the taste of cash
(whilst knitting sweaters for chillest regulatory weather)
they surge the arteries of capital in quiet ranks—
their shoals swim grand and deep in the richest banks
between the teeth of creatures of gilt-embossed leather—
waltzing the halls of power with such panache
they're sure they'll trump whatever their foes concoct.
A tasty merge, a full-bodied acquire, delight
the gentle esquires . . . they do not mind if their churning,
mounding papers scratch out lives and disappear Peru—
it's just a matter of defining the sky as blue
outside their suites . . . so what if a far away wind is turning
so dry no tears can fall on the bones at night.

Dear Marcel

(after *White Cabinet and White Table*, Marcel Broodthaers, 1965)

I face your white and I am white
I disappear, blood let, enshrouded
cloud out blots everything
I ever thought, white out.

Cupboard of stuffed space
an asphyxiation of delicately shelled air
behind closed doors but visible, beckoning
swelling lungs to its rectangular hold.

Table encrusted with air
the breakable kind, painted
white, of course, for nothingness
reverse transubstantiation, eat this for it is
without content other than the air.

A hundred hundred calciferous ovals
privatized, unavailable, white hoard
what had contained life, lifeless—
a madman's eucharist.

My white arm reaches out
mouth open and soundless
I cannot stop my arm, not knowing
even what it intends to do—
when it breaks off I am not surprised.

I turn my head to see if you are paying attention
my brittle neck cracks, a head, on collision
split apart on the floor.

Nothing there but air.

On Not Knowing

Carry your ambivalence confidently, both
hands bright, a fool everywhere but—
                      stop here—
grab the feathered meter. Guts
        hang out, tongue
                lolling. Such confidence the plate

shatters. You were fooling and it's not
        funny.   The house is on fire. You
piss in the wind. Where then is home? Whose
table do you set with shattered plates? You offer
                your confidence, palms up, but
                              leaning too far forward.
It is instead now unmentionable.

Everyone turns away. An indifferent wind translates
        the landscape, the old side table now
                a pile of dirt. Where are you? It is so
                        hard to tell anymore. You tiptoe
around the rooms, abandoned, bread-crumbing.

I Am Never Ready for This

Babble babble babble. Opposite parties nod. Laughter.
Communication articulated.
The solitary finds a moment = relief. Other parties pass through.
Opening? Shut. When is attention earned? Not understood.
Speaking attempted.... *smell of pedantic garrulity.*
The solitary in community = conundrum.

I am never ready for this.

Inner meter + outer actor do not align. The solitary = conundrum,
i.e. failure to communicate.
Other speaks. Connection + the solitary = inability to align, *i.e.*
       perception of invasion.
My coldness in company has justifiably deprived me of the goodwill of many.
Failure to communicate meaning clumsy,
meaning attempt = incorrect somatic feedback.
Conundrum = pretend this is going well = it is not.
Party turns away, *i.e.* perception as predator.

I am never ready for this. However
      ... quality of self cannot be maintained by imitating
the natures of others and neglecting our own.
And yet....

Babble babble babble babble SMILE babble babble babble. Outside
and inside are confusing.

      ... innate difficulty in giving ... by halves and with reservations, and
with that slavish and suspicious prudence that is required of us in the conduct of
our numerous and imperfect friendships.

The solitary seeks, *i.e.* closes door, *i.e.* closes door.
    The companionship of books ... is much more certain....
And yet.

Community, meaning many + the solitary ÷ silence ≥ try again.
Open door, enter room. Articulate communication. Babble smile.
   Outside ≠ inside.

My Name is Martín

(Martín Ramírez, 1895 - 1963. Immigrating from Mexico, he worked on the California railroads from 1925-1930. He ended up unemployed and homeless which led to him being detained by police and institutionalized, diagnosed with schizophrenia, leaning towards catatonia. A self-taught artist, Ramirez spent over 30 years in California state hospitals where he made the drawings and collages for which he is now known.)

I have my wooden mouth sticks they are mine. I have my pencils they
    are mine.
I have crayons and paints they are mine. I take these magazines they
    are mine.
No scissors no scissors I carefully tear so precise. I make and I make
    and I make.

It pleases me.

I am in a box I look around me out of the box out into the world.

I see in lines.

Inside my mind runs in lines. I run the lines of my mind out
into the world and onto the paper. Stripes.

I see what I see.

You are saying many things but I see what I see
streaming, everything streaming.

I make myself on paper. Myself gets bigger so I make
the paper bigger. I mash up the potato that I hid from my
meal. I mix it with spit and smear the paper, glue it to another
paper, it grows to bigger paper so I can complete myself on paper,

the lines and streams of color.

You say so many things it falls on me like rain. I do not like the rain.
I hide under my thoughts until you stop. I have nothing to say to you.

I spit and my pictures grow.

The Unbanked

We were seeing check-cashing places pop up on every corner, and thought, you know, we're a bank—we can do that better than they can do that. So why wouldn't we get into this business and really approach the un-banked as a market segment?
—Interview heard on the radio

Drifting through dishes and breakfast on burbling
        broadcast voices, I slide right onto the razored word
so nonchalantly cast into the stream, I'm hooked.
        Unbanked?

Mind chafing on chilly bland construct, I pull up reflecting,
        sifting the layers of this nominative predation:
        the unbanked.

        un: to reverse, to deprive or remove

Eagles are opportunists, no picky dietary restrictions for them
with their giggling cries. Should the opportunity arise,
        eat it!

I ponder the comforts of being banked as the word
        ripples out in multiple directions—

Bank the boat. Pull it up out of wild current, look back
        see the drowning ones sluiced away.

Bank the coals, embers buried in their own ash,
        snug, holding their small fire through the night
tomorrow to be hot and bright so food and hands
        will be warmed, filled, secure.

The mountebank counts his check-cashing fees, rubbing hands. Smiling signage offers what you can't refuse. You have no other options.

                        You are unbanked.

Visiting Gettysburg National Military Park

Walk across, the green lying there, a green blanket tucked in at rock and wall, here rumpled, here flat, inviting the eye lying, lying here on a hot Pennsylvania summer day.

the last full measure

*　　*　　*

Équilibre du plateau the school in Paris called it, training body and mind. Imagine a geometrical plane. Imagine it balanced on a single point. Make two groups and move on the plane. Imagine keeping it in balance, each group eyeing the other, countering, feinting . . .

our fathers brought forth . . . that that nation

*　　*　　*

Vertigo ensues despite it all being in your head.
Imaginary tilting. Imaginary stakes.
Tipping. Felt. Carnival ride, Tilt O' Whirl, Teacups, Octopus . . .

the proposition that . . . little note nor long remember . . . devotion

*　　*　　*

Landscape lies. Green plane stretched out under sun.
Our bodies stuck in the postcard present.
Little rumple of simple, unimportant thoughts. Sky pinned in the middle by tree. Point of turning.
Silent standing Z-axis of this space, this time . . .

Time turns, runs up and down. No third axis until—
        that buzzing—

Humming horsefly flips the switch, green plateau
tips, flitting swallowtail rides the steaming
dead, drills us through to
        the maggoty boy, fallen

    we cannot . . . we cannot . . . we cannot . . . this ground

Vertiginous nausea, spin and tilt, hot air sucked through
horse snot and lather, sweat of wool-clad frenzy, gray-
and-blue thunder hoof hit fire cannon sweat wet—
        no—blood . . .
            torn off bleeding live flesh
                              soon dead,
the wet moaning . . .

    little note nor long remember . . . hallow . . . this ground

The Angle. Two lines meet. Degrees. Two histories meet.
Picture postcard trees, summer green now so quiet.

    the proposition that . . . equal

        *   *   *

Our little life—we visit our history,
stroll through the town, rub against the local,
finger the merchandise not really looking at the price.

    unfinished work . . . fitting and proper . . . the living

Visitors fan out in random groups over the surface.
The land, lying quiet, outweighs them.

    conceived in liberty . . . shall not perish

The bloodied field tilted that day. What if,
    in the agony,
it had spun the other way. . .

Nullus Casus Belli

<blockquote>(after Balthus, Still Life with a Figure, 1940)</blockquote>

Dusk. Onset. Coming of more than darkness.
Freighted chariots catastrophying
two valleys distant. How simple shrinks
to spare. Knife cuts last year's crop—open

cracks in everything. Draping over the table, the rich
daubs, glints, pull focus to our fingertips, our now
wet mouths. Distracted from the unimaginable.
Storm? The dead laugh. Cracking, I reach
to flat. Stroke. Point. Ground. Glaze. Frame.

Behind our backs the world is flaking off
into worse than nothing. Leaning forward
forward, aching for the smell, bread and apples.
Tiny patch of dawn—is it possible?—on her cheek.

What the Poem Wants

The poem is lying on the sidewalk and wishes you would pick it up.
The poem wants dissonant lineation and enjambent.
The poem wants to contraindicate and catalog.
The poem wants you to be a good girl.

The poem wants to be the armature on which you hang yourself.
The poem wants two eggs over easy and a side of bacon.
The poem wants a place at the table.
The poem wants a thin film wrapping its soft parts.

The poem wants some damn good conversation.
The poem wants to hide the answer.

The poem wants to be rescued.
The poem wants iambs with or without pentameter.
"Watch where you're stepping," shouts the poem, "that's my foot!"
The poem wants a donut but knows it will feel sick after.

The poem wants to change everything.
The poem wants to stay the same.
The poem wants to rhyme AND to scheme.
A-B-A-B! C-D-C-D! cries the poem.
The poem wants some social grace.

The poem wants to be read between the lines.
"Anapest Budapest trochee spondEE," chants the young poem,
jumping rope.
The poem wants another way to count.

The poem wants the reverberation of the finite in the infinite to be in
lines 12-14.
The poem wants to distinguish grapes from bananas.
The poem wants to kill things.
The poem wants to run away.

The poem wants you to stop thinking so hard and listen.
The poem wants to sound like more than it means.
The poem wants to mean more than it looks like it should.
The poem wants to be peeled like a hard-boiled egg.
The poem is worn down by interpretation.
The poem wants a nap.

The poem wants privacy.
The poem wants to stand despite all possibilities of falling.
The poem wants to observe what goes unnoticed by everyone else.
The poem vows devotion to small things.
The poem wants to learn to fly a plane.

The poem wants active lines, even if limited by fixed points.
The poem wants to be left alone to do as it pleases.
The poem wants to be held on your tongue.

River Song in the Shape of the Hudson

Vasty river god, in rock time lies abed
sleeping and glassy, one seagull.
Crack! new stripe, a slide spills
light down the cliff. Rockfall.

River god clenches still at his loss—
daughter chased by god, his wild
girl trapped at river's edge. No
other help but loss. Please!
River's watery pour crashes,
bright charm spins deep.
Girl knots shut, skeined
in bark—daughter now
tree.

The cliff, too, has changed,
will change again. Sweet
girl's loss does not. He
expected softening—
it has not come.

Currents shift and change.
Tides wash the heart
into a clean bone—
loss the single
shining
thing.

I lie in bed
stare at the wall.
All the city's dirt
leaves its testimony
on sills, cracks filled
with soot, once-white
paint scrubbed to
an unknowable color.

I drift
on current.
For now it lies deep
running in
near silence.

Train and truck
traffic sing
outside. Today
my river is not singing,
it's not yelling at me
or following my nudges. Do you
remember? I ask. It only
wants to go back to sleep.

Let's sleep, it says. You're tired.
You can stay in bed and sleep. I
don't answer. I keep my eyes open.

Incantation for a Bad Day

"One-dimensional thought is systematically promoted by the makers of politics and their purveyors of mass information. Their universe of discourse is populated by self validating hypotheses which, incessantly [...] repeated, become hypnotic definitions [...]. For example, 'free'..."

—Herbert Marcuse

On the bad days, writing a poem seems incredibly stupid, a self-indulgent waste of time. The best poets are writing the best poems all perfectly published and every other person you pass on the street fancies themselves bardic, so why bother. You sit there beetle-browed fingering your hopelessness as though it instead of you were in charge.

The bad days are legion, little bad days and big bad days, Despair pleasuring herself in the corner flashing her wet broken grin, Stupor quick to follow, whatever the formulary, eyelids flaccid, drooping soul, pencil abandoned on the nightstand with the empty glass as you pull the covers over your head.

Yes, things are bad, a bad thing happens and there is much flapping of hands and exclaiming. A real case of the vapours, but what do you expect? You're not going to let that fool you, are you? Can you really be so easily shut down when the bad ones come snooping around and shit on your lawn?

Think past the bad things, Horatio, you know them, know them so well you could puke. That boy with the guns was damaged goods, a rupture in the wiring, the high voltage raging of violence exploding through defective harness.

Meanwhile the keepers of the gate to the Fort Knox of the lockdown of the inner sanctum of where the violence comes from, how happy are they at all the jabbering about the shooting boy? Real, real happy as they turn up the juice of their hypocrisy, the wet broken violence running down their chins.

That man at the top is a bad bad man, sanctimonious and a liar and his friends are even worse. They'd slam your head in the locker and then smarm the teacher, who always falls for it. The bad men hoard their badness, jingling it in their pockets—they're bullies, they're greedy and now they can slam the whole goddamn planet in the locker which they do without thinking twice.

The worst little club in the world, they sit there stoking the fires, lying and smiling and pulling the wings off flies and their fire heats the cauldron that steams the engine that powers the generator of bad things. The roaring flames suck the oxygen from our lungs and scarify the land as the generator shunts its evil through the grid and no one notices because of the broken boy who sprayed out a real tragedy for sure but if you get stuck on him, you're facing in the wrong direction—look upstream, Malvolio, or they've got you by the short hairs!

Your rant is meaningless, you say, how do we get from murder to poetry? That is the question. It's the bad men's words, Newton, the slow drip, one for the Gip, wipe your lip 'cause you're drooling, cowboy, they upped the dosage while you were clicking the remote, your hand in your pants and your mouth full of chips.

The political beauty parlors are ironing it all flat, kiddo, crippling the nation while you wallow in your melancholy. Remember the butterfly's wing, Bluto, each breathless flap, each pen prick lifts apart a couple of words stuck together by the spittle of evil from the bad bad men and their wet broken minds.

So instead of blowing yourself up—decant the bad spells that have all our heads in a vise. Make a word, then a word, arc crackling in between, just a little ink-grunting every day, Mehitabel. *Toujours gai* is my motto, kid, which I especially have to remind myself of on a really bad day.

Realization While Trying to Live as a Late 16th c. Japanese Warrior

There are many details in the art of preemption but they cannot fully be written down because. . .
    —Musashi, *Book of Five Rings*

Because as lines glide, preemption flies to follow them.
Because the land snail and the sea snail both have merit in their song.
Because everyone in your immediate vicinity is either an idiot or not available at this time.
Because your opponent is often disguised as your friend (preemptive preemption—ha).
Because the cunning response to idiocy is silence.
Because the grownups' table doesn't exist.
Because the bluestone step holds the impression of 365-million-year-old raindrops.
Because the sheer whatever of it opens wide letting words fly off the page.
Because, let's face it,
      you've rarely successfully
                      preempted anything.

Yours is the art of postemption.
         There are many details in the art of postemption.
                      —I am writing them down.

Postemption is a pound up and a penny sorry.
Postemption follows a tune no snail recognizes.
Postemption relies on subtle theories that explain the wrong topic.
Postemption wants to sit at the grownups' table. See above.
Postemption flies in the face of convention. Someone breaks a tooth.
Postemption reads social cues which unfortunately only apply in an alternate universe.
Postemption dots the land of unrequited admiration, mistaken identities, opportunities missed.

Postemption is fatigue, the mopping up after I told you so, tending
    the wounds, words
                    bandaging weariness . . .
                                    and it just bleeds out as it will.

        Post post post . . .
                    aftershave aftertaste aftermath afterlife after . . .
        What postemptors pick their way through between the
            preemptors' footsteps.

Walked into a Bar

A strict, a loose, a detailed and an ambiguous
housekeeper walked into a bar.

Loose was lost right off the nibs. "Not
necessary," she shouted into her drink.

Detailed was counting coasters and stacking them
(in perfect piles, of course) while Ambiguous
wafted around the room sitting in one chair,
then another, then talking to the oracle
on the pay telephone in the corner.

Strict cocked her pistol. Bang! Bang!
went the toy flag which she carefully
rolled back up and stashed in the barrel
of her gun. "I'll have what she's having,"
says Loose from up near the ceiling
where she was picking dead flies
from the fol-de-rol fan blades.

"White out! White out!" cried Detailed
who by now had covered the bar in coasters.
Whose details were they anyway?

The mysteries of keeping, the mysteries
of house—each keeper kept each house-
keeping plate on its pole, spinning.

Notes

First, some thoughts: I have mixed feelings about notes to poetry collections. Sometimes I am happy they are there. Sometimes not. But placed at the end of the book, reading them is optional. I appreciate notes that translate foreign phrases or technical terms, attribute quoted text or explain an obscure reference. Some notes might describe the source or starting point of a poem. Bottom line, poem-making is hard to pull apart. Poetry and its craft are threaded through with mysteries of the creative process and how little we understand about it. So describing backstory will either illuminate and add something to the reader's experience or not. But again, reading them is optional. All of that said, I'm opting for a notes section. Please feel free to skim it or ignore it as suits you. I have provided some translation, some background information and a few stories about origins and associations for particular poems.

I also would like to acknowledge an important learning experience. I once took a workshop that I really, really, really didn't like. The group chemistry, the assignments, the style of critiquing work, all felt both dull and unhelpful. We were assigned the task of "imitating" various poems handed out by the teacher (an instruction open to wide interpretation). I had no idea what I was doing, but as I struggled, I found bouncing off other people's poems to be extremely productive. I did not use the poet's words, but the structure, lineation and rhythms of a particular poem—a kind of ekphrasis. So thank you to the poets whose work I trampolined off of. And thank you to the workshop I so disliked for teaching me about just shutting up and writing.

And now the specific notes, by section:

I

"Prognostics of Melancholy"—Robert Burton (1577–1640) is perhaps less well known today, but admirers of his "Anatomy of Melancholy" include Laurence Sterne, Samuel Johnson, Benjamin Franklin, John Keats, William Osler, and Samuel Beckett. And me.

Pierre Bonnard—In 1925, after 32 years together, Bonnard married his mistress and muse, Marthe. She appears in many of Bonnard's paintings. *The Bathroom* from 1932 (q.v. moma.org) is a personal favorite of mine. Marthe died in 1942. In 1944, Bonnard wrote in his diary, "He who sings is not always happy." Come 1946, in *Cooking Utensils*, a narrow, from-the-back edge of Bonnard's face anchors the lower right corner of this atypically (for Bonnard) dark painting. I may be making it up, but I see an arc from the tactile and luminous beauty of *The Bathroom* to the hanging implements in the wife-less kitchen of *Cooking Utensils*. Bonnard died the next year.

"Space—Counter Space"—In a social studies class a million years ago, we were shown the famous documentary about the Army-McCarthy hearings. I will never forget attorney Joseph Welch finally saying to Senator Joseph McCarthy, with an understated exasperation, "Have you no decency, sir?" Thinking about it years later, I misremembered the name of the documentary as *Point/Counterpoint*. The documentary was actually called *Point of Order* but the other title kept jangling around in my head. In addition, New York's Museum of Modern Art had a fascinating show called *Counter Space: Design and the Modern Kitchen*. Hence "Space—Counter Space." What does this all mean? Nothing except that there is a world of inchoate memories, misremembrances, accidents and juxtapositions that can go into the making of a poem.

"Nightmare for Theodore Roethke"—in his essay "The Teaching Poet" (from *On the Poet and his Craft*), Roethke suggests a series of exercises, one of which is to make a poem based on adjectives. That generated this poem, which was published by *The Gettysburg Review*. Thank you, Roethke.

"Behavioral Game Theory": *The brain doesn't like ambiguous situations. When it can't figure out what is happening, the amygdala transmits fear to the orbitofrontal cortex*. Italicized quote is from Colin Camerer.

"Necessary"—outfall of an arbitrary exercise: pick a random word from the dictionary, then use it to make an acrostic poem (i.e each letter of the chosen word begins a line of the poem).

II

"Take and Fold"—a teacher I once had literally gave us a list of words to *never* use in a poem. This poem uses *all* those words. "Some Trees" is the title of John Ashbery's first book of poems.

"Boolean Search"—does anyone use Boolean searching anymore? It seems like everything has devolved to natural language search. Overall, that's probably a good thing. But Boolean searching is kind of cool. It uses operators (like AND, OR and NOT) with parentheses for grouping. It is reminiscent of algebra, which I always enjoyed and was pretty good at which is probably why I like Boolean searching.

"Relation/Couch/Dreaming"—my ekphrastic response to an untitled drawing by Morris Yarowsky from 1966. I have this drawing because my late husband was a colleague and friend of Yarowsky's (long before we met). The drawing hangs on a wall in my living space. I never tire of looking at it.

"*Heimisch*"—a German word, as defined in Cassell's German dictionary "*adj*. home, domestic". I like to frame it as *heim* means home so *heimisch* is homish (not a real word, but you get the idea) Its Yiddish definition is "domestic, home-made, cozy, snug, familiar, intimate, informal". The Dutch were the first Europeans to settle western Long Island. They named their settlement *Breuckelen* later anglicized to Brookland, then eventually becoming Brooklyn (q.v. *Broken land: Poems of Brooklyn*, ed. Julia Spicher Kasdorf & Michael Tyrell). *Geh weiter weg!* means go farther way. This is a punchline from a comedy routine mixing Yiddish and English (I believe it was Mickey Katz, Joel Grey's father) that we had on an LP when I was a kid. (The whole phrase was *Geh weg—geh weiter weg*, or "Go away—go farther away"). I only remember this phrase because my father was always repeating it with great hilarity.

"In the Beginning" after Robert Penn Warren's "Evening Hawk"

"My Sweet Conjunct"—*Dies süsse Wörtlein:* **und** means "This sweet little word: *and*." For context, in Act II, Sc. 2 of Richard Wagner's *Tristan und Isolde*, Isolde sings:
> But our love,
> is it not Tristan
> *and* Isolde?
> This sweet little word: *and*,
> would death not destroy
> the bonds of love
> which it entwines
> if Tristan were to die?

"Foxtrot"—after Dean Young's "Sunflower"

"Countless"—italic sections are excerpted from Wikipedia articles *Suprasternal Notch*, *Skin* and *Calendar*.

"Sweat"—after Tony Hoagland's "Jet"

"Roadside Turnout—Scenic View Area"—*Ignorantia juris non excusat:* ignorance of the law is not an excuse.

III

"Merge and Acquire"—after e.e. cummings' "the Cambridge ladies who live in furnished souls"

"Dear Marcel"—ekphrastic on *White Cabinet and White Table*, Marcel Broodthaers, 1965 (in the collection of the Museum of Modern Art, New York, q.v. moma.org)

"I Am Never Ready for This"—italics are quotes from essays of Michel de Montaigne.

"My Name is Martín"—from an exhibition of the works of Martín Ramirez seen at the American Folk Art Museum in New York City (q.v. folkartmuseum.org).

"Visiting Gettysburg National Military Park"—italics in English are quotes from Abraham Lincoln's "Gettysburg Address." *Équilibre du plateau* translates as "balancing the plane," a wonderful class exercise I practiced at the Lecoq School in Paris. Two groups face off and as one group moves, the other has to compensate to keep the (imaginary) tipping plane level.

Nullus Casus Belli: after Balthus, *Still Life with a Figure*, 1940. The term usually heard is *casus belli* (an act or event that provokes or is used to justify war, *i.e.* a cause or case for war). When the Germans invaded France in June 1940, the painter Balthus fled Paris to Champrovent, a small village in the French Alps. Here he painted *Still Life with a Figure 1940* (by 1942 he had left France entirely for Switzerland). The simple stuffs of the painting—bread, apples, the farmer's young daughter—in the context of the encroaching German invasion seemed to me a striking argument against war, hence *nullus casus belli* or no case for war. (in the collection of the Tate Museum, q.v. www.tate.org.uk/art/artworks/klossowski-de-rola-still-life-with-a-figure-t12613)

About the Author

Diane Schenker is author of the chapbook "Relation/Couch/Dreaming" (Finishing Line Press). "Expert Terrain" was shortlisted by the Harbor Mountain Press MURA Book Award and was given Honorable Mention by the Concrete Wolf Louis Poetry Book Award. Her most recent poems appear in "Pen + Brush In Print No. 4." Previous publications are in "The Gettysburg Review," "Rhino," "Subtropics," "Gargoyle" and the annual review published by the Community of Writers at Olympic Valley, among others. She has been a fellow at The Gettysburg Review Conference for Writers and is a two-time alum of the Community of Writers summer poetry workshop. She has read at various venues around New York City including The Center for Book Arts, Sunday Salon and KGB Bar.

In a first iteration of her life, Diane worked and taught extensively in theater and directed opera. She was a company member at The Empty Space Theater in Seattle and a founding member of the theater faculty at Cornish College of the Arts. She created and performed in *Jane Smith Jane Smith* and *Nannerl: A Speculative Morality* at On the Boards in Seattle.

Diane's parents hailed from Brooklyn and the Bronx, but when her father (with an electrical engineering degree from Cooper Union) took a job in the Berkshires, she was born in Williamstown, MA. When she was 8 years old, they moved again and then again as her dad went through a period of changing employers. They were briefly near Cape Cod, then Chicago for a couple of years, then to San Francisco's South Bay Area where the family finally settled. After high school, Diane attended the University of Washington, graduating with a B.A. in drama followed by two years of study in Paris at the *École Jacques Lecoq*. She then returned to Seattle to pursue opportunities in theater (see "first iteration" above). After moving to New York City in 1993 (her ancestral home from which she was banished before she was born), she directed multiple pieces for the American Chamber Opera Company, did a few out-of-town gigs, but ultimately transitioned from making theater to making words on a page into poetry. She now happily reads and writes in upstate Manhattan.